Editor
Erica N. Russikoff, M.A.

Editor in Chief
Karen J. Goldfluss, M.S. Ed.

Creative Director
Sarah M. Fournier

Cover Artist
Barb Lorseyedi

Illustrator
Kelly McMahon

Art Coordinator
Renée Mc Elwee

Imaging
Craig Gunnell

Publisher
Mary D. Smith, M.S. Ed.

Celebrating
Reading, Writing & Hands-on Activities

★ Focuses on more than 20 holidays
★ Includes a description of each holiday, as well as reading, writing, and speaking & listening activities
★ Provides vocabulary related to each holiday
★ Contains activities correlated to the Common Core State Standards

Teacher Created Resources

Author
Julia McMeans, M. Ed.

CORRELATED TO
COMMON CORE
STANDARDS

For correlations to the Common Core State Standards, see pages 127–128. Correlations can also be found at *http://www.teachercreated.com/standards.*

Teacher Created Resources
6421 Industry Way
Westminster, CA 92683
www.teachercreated.com
ISBN: 978-1-4206-3033-6
© 2015 Teacher Created Resources
Made in U.S.A.

Teacher Created Resources

Table of Contents

Introduction

Happy holidays! *Celebrating Holidays* was developed to help you introduce, teach, and celebrate the holidays with your students, whether you are new to the classroom or an experienced teacher. This book is full of original fiction, poetry, and nonfiction, along with speaking, listening, writing, and craft activities that will help you get the holiday celebrations started. And the best thing about these activities is that they were written for the reading grade level of your students and are aligned to the Common Core State Standards.

Common Core-Aligned Activities

All of the reading passages and the activities that accompany them align to specific directives within the Common Core. For example, there is an emphasis on activities that are text-dependent, meaning students must look for details in the text itself, as opposed to sharing opinions, making deductions, and drawing inferences. It's not that the latter is not present; it's just that there has been a shift in focus.

Accommodating Younger Readers

Although all of the reading passages meet the grades 1—2 Flesch-Kincaid levels, some of the texts may be difficult or lengthy for these younger readers. Consider reading these sections aloud. Alternatively, you can ask parents to read to their children.

Providing Context

While this book covers many important holidays celebrated in the United States, you should provide additional context in order for your students to get a full appreciation of each holiday.

Consider having a discussion with your students about the significance of holidays and celebrations in general as a component of culture. Encourage students to think about the broader benefits of large-scale celebrations to the community and country. Make sure that they understand that people everywhere have customs and traditions, and that while those may differ from our own, they are just as meaningful for those cultures.

Holidays are a mirror of the society in which they are celebrated. They reflect a people's deepest-held convictions and reveal the beliefs, values, desires, and—ultimately—the sacrifices that a society is willing to make.

How to Use This Book

This book is divided into 22 units. Each unit covers a specific holiday. The holidays are arranged chronologically, beginning with New Year's Day and ending with Kwanzaa, although some holiday dates change from year to year.

Each unit contains the following:

- a holiday description to be shared with students
- a summary of the activities within the unit
- a literature reading activity
- an informational text reading activity
- a writing activity
- a bonus (craft) or speaking & listening activity
- suggested vocabulary: These are words that students will encounter either by reading a passage or simply by discussing the holiday. You might want to consider introducing these words before you begin the unit. Some of the vocabulary is repetitive as it applies to more than one holiday.

Here is a sample description and summary:

Groundhog Day

February 2

Will he or won't he? Phil is a groundhog. He has a special job. On February 2, he leaves his burrow. He takes a good look around. If Phil sees his shadow, it means six more weeks of winter. If he doesn't see it, it means that spring will come early.

Summary of Activities

Reading: Literature
The Shy Groundhog—fictional story with a writing prompt

Reading: Informational Text
Animal Fact File—nonfiction passage with comprehension questions

Writing
Show What You Know—graphic-organizer activity

Speaking & Listening
A Groundhog Is Also a Woodchuck—tongue-twister activity

Vocabulary: burrow, hibernate, shadow, woodchuck

New Year's Day
The First Day of the Year—January 1

Happy New Year! That is what people say on New Year's Day. New Year's Day is the first day of the year. It is a fun day. Most people do not go to work or school on this day. There are parades on New Year's Day. It is a time to think about the future.

Summary of Activities

Reading: Literature
The Parade—fictional story with a drawing activity

Reading: Informational Text
What to Eat on New Year's Day—nonfiction passage with comprehension questions

Writing
Setting Goals—activity in which students write New Year's resolutions

Speaking & Listening
Looking Forward to New Year's Day—activity in which students share personal experiences about New Year's Day

Vocabulary: celebrate, goal, holiday, parade, resolutions

Name_____   Date _____

The Parade

Directions: Read the story. Then complete the activity.

Sam was happy. He was at his first New Year's Day parade! He was with his dad. Sam's dad lifted him way up. Sam saw loud marching bands. Sam saw funny clowns. Sam even saw a man dressed up to look like a baby. Sam asked why a man was dressed like that.

"He is like the New Year," Sam's dad said. "He has just been born!"

All the people at the parade were having fun. They were saying, "Happy New Year!"

"That's what you say on New Years Day," Sam's dad said.

Sam felt shy about saying it. He had never wished anyone a Happy New Year before. But then he saw his friend, John. John was with his dad, too.

John's dad said "Happy New Year" to Sam's dad. They shook hands.

Then John said "Happy New Year" to Sam. Sam looked up at his dad. His dad smiled at him. Then Sam looked at John.

"Happy New Year, John," Sam said.

Sam and John shook hands just like their dads did. And the four of them watched the rest of the parade together.

Activity: Draw a picture of the story. Make sure that your picture shows where the story happens and who the characters are.

Name_____   Date _____

What to Eat on New Year's Day

Directions: Read the passage. Then answer the questions.

New Year's Day is the start of a new year. People hope that they will have a good year. They hope that they will be lucky.

There are some foods that some people believe might bring you good luck in the New Year. These are the foods that they think you should eat on New Year's Day. There are other foods that they think might bring you bad luck. These are the foods that they think you should not eat on New Year's Day.

Good Luck Foods

① Eat long noodles. They can bring you a long life. Be careful! Don't break the noodle before you have the whole thing in your mouth!

② Eat black-eyed peas. They are thought to bring you lots of good luck. Some say you should eat one for every day in the year.

③ Eat cabbage. It is green. It is the same color as money. If you eat cabbage, you may make lots of money!

Bad Luck Foods

① Do not eat lobster. Lobsters move backward. You do not want your life to move backward.

② Do not eat birds. Some say that if you eat a bird, your luck will fly away.

---

1. How are long noodles and cabbage the same?

   a. They are both unlucky foods.
   b. They are both lucky foods.
   c. They are both green.

2. Which one should you **not** eat on New Year's Day?

   a. chicken
   b. noodles
   c. cabbage

3. What is the passage about?

   a. what to eat or not eat on New Year's Day
   b. black-eyed peas
   c. money

Name_____ **Date** _____

Setting Goals

On New Year's Day, people plan for the year ahead. They think about things that they would like to do. They think about what they would like to change. People can make a list of these things. These things are called *resolutions*. They are goals.

Now, it's your turn. Pretend it is New Year's Day. What are your goals? What are some things that you would like to do? What are some things that you would like to change?

Write your three goals here. Make sure your sentences begin with capital letters and end with periods.

1. _____

_____

_____

_____

2. _____

_____

_____

_____

3. _____

_____

_____

_____

Name_____ **Date** _____

Looking Forward to New Year's Day

Tell a true story to your classmates about what your family does on New Year's Day.

OR

Share with your classmates what you are looking forward to doing on the next New Year's Day.

Martin Luther King, Jr. Day
The Third Monday of January

Martin Luther King, Jr. was an African American leader. He was also the head of a church. He fought for the rights of African Americans. He wanted all people to be treated the same. He was a peaceful man. He led marches to help people win their rights. He died doing what he believed. We do not go to school or work on Martin Luther King, Jr. Day. We honor what he did. We work together in our communities.

Summary of Activities

Reading: Literature
The Lot—fictional story with a sequencing activity

Reading: Informational Text
Helping Out—nonfiction passage with comprehension questions

Writing
Giving Back—activity in which students write about volunteering

Speaking & Listening
Helping Others—activity in which students share personal experiences about helping friends or family members

Vocabulary: African American, civil rights, communities, volunteer

Name _____ **Date** _____

The Lot

Directions: Read the story. Then complete the activity on page 12.

It was a cold Monday morning. Kate was glad that school was closed. All she wanted to do was stay warm in her bed. But it was Martin Luther King, Jr. Day. Kate had a feeling that her mom would make her get up and help out.

Kate sat down at the kitchen table. She ate her breakfast.

"Do I have to go?" Kate asked.

"You know the answer to that," Kate's mom said.

"But it's cold, and that old lot is full of trash. Can't somebody else help clean it up?"

"Well, guess what your name is going to be today?" Kate's mom asked.

Kate looked up from her toast.

"Miss Somebody Else!"

Kate and her mom walked down to the lot. There were already people there. Kate knew most of them. Some were her friends from school. Others were people who lived nearby. Mr. Green got everyone in a circle.

"Today, we are here to honor Dr. King. This isn't a day off. It's a day on! We will do as Dr. King did. We will come together. We will work together."

Kate and her mom put on work gloves. They began to pick up the trash all over the lot. Others raked dry leaves. A group of boys gave an old fence a fresh coat of paint.

After an hour, the sun came out. It warmed up. People started to chat as they worked. Some girls that Kate knew from school came over. They asked if Kate could work with them.

"Sure," Kate's mom said. Kate ran away with the group of girls laughing.

At the end of the day, Mr. Green called everyone together again in a circle. Kate stood next to her mom, who took her hand.

"Take a look around, folks. Look at what we did here today."

Everyone looked at the lot. The trash was gone. The fence and all the benches had been painted. There was even a new swing set.

Name_____   Date _____

The Lot (cont.)

Directions: Read the story beginning on page 11. Then complete the activity.

Everyone smiled at each other and shook hands. They all felt good about what they had done.

Kate and her mom walked home, holding hands.

"Well, what do you think?" Kate's mom asked.

Kate smiled. "I think that I'm glad I didn't stay in bed this morning!"

Activity: The pictures below tell parts of the story. Cut out these pictures. Tape the pictures onto a piece of yarn in the order that they happened in the story.

12   ©Teacher Created Resources

Name_____   Date _____

Helping Out

Directions: Read the passage. Then answer the questions.

Earning Money

There are two kinds of work that you can do. Some work you do to earn money. Do you clean up your room? Do you do other things to help out? Maybe your mom or dad pays you to do small jobs around the house. It is good to work to earn money.

Volunteering

There is another kind of work that you can do. This is work that you do not get paid for. You do it just to help. When you do this kind of work, you are called a volunteer. A volunteer is a person who works for free. It is good to do this kind of work, too!

How to Help

There are lots of ways that you can volunteer. Do you like animals? Animal shelters need people to care for the cats and dogs. Do you like to be outside? You could help to clean up a park. Do you like to talk to older people? You could go to a nursing or retirement home to spend some time with older folks.

New Friends, New Skills

When you volunteer, you meet new people. It is a good way to make new friends. When you volunteer, you can learn a new skill. It is fun to learn to do new things. When you volunteer, you help others. This is the best part of all!

1. What work could you do to earn money?
   a. wash the dishes   **b.** ride your bicycle   **c.** volunteer

2. Volunteer means that
   a. you get paid for your work.   **b.** you work for free.   **c.** you earn money.

3. Why is it good to volunteer?
   a. You earn money.   **b.** It is easy.   **c.** You help others.

Name_____   **Date** _____

Giving Back

Martin Luther King, Jr. Day is a day to help others. It is a day to help around where you live. There are lots of ways that you can do this. You don't have to wait until this special day to help out. You can help at any time.

Think about how and whom you would like to help. What are some things you would like to do?

Write three ways you would like to help. Make sure to begin your sentences with capital letters and end them with periods.

1. _____

_____

_____

_____

2. _____

_____

_____

_____

3. _____

_____

_____

_____

Name_____ **Date** _____

Helping Others

Think about a time when you helped someone. Maybe you helped a family member with something around the house. Or maybe you did something for a friend.

How did it feel to help someone? Share your story with a classmate.

Groundhog Day

February 2

Will he or won't he? Phil is a groundhog. He has a special job. On February 2, he leaves his burrow. He takes a good look around. If Phil sees his shadow, it means six more weeks of winter. If he doesn't see it, it means that spring will come early.

Summary of Activities

Reading: Literature
The Shy Groundhog—fictional story with a writing prompt

Reading: Informational Text
Animal Fact File—nonfiction passage with comprehension questions

Writing
Show What You Know—graphic-organizer activity

Speaking & Listening
A Groundhog Is Also a Woodchuck—tongue-twister activity

Vocabulary: burrow, hibernate, shadow, woodchuck

Name_____   **Date** _____

The Shy Groundhog

Directions: Read the story. Then complete the activity.

Phil looked at the date and sighed. It was February 1. Each year, it was the same. Phil knew that on February 2, he had a job to do. He would have to leave his warm burrow and go out into the cold winter air. There would be crowds of people. All the people in the town would stare at him. Phil didn't like this at all. He was a very shy groundhog.

Now, Phil had a twin brother named Fred. No one could tell them apart. And Fred was not shy at all. He loved having his picture taken!

"I have an idea," said Phil to Fred. "How about if you be me just for the day?"

"Oh, I don't know," said Fred. "Wouldn't that be cheating?"

"Well, sort of. But no one but us will know."

Fred loved his brother. He knew how much he hated to be in front of all those people. He wanted to help.

"O.K.," said Fred. "But you will have to teach me how to look for my shadow."

That whole day, Phil showed his brother what to do.

"First, you walk out of the burrow," Phil said. "Next, you look to your left. Then, you look to your right."

Fred did what his brother said. He walked out of the burrow. He looked to his left and then to his right.

"I can't see my shadow," said Fred. "Am I doing something wrong?"

"No," said Phil. "If it is cloudy, you won't be able to see your shadow. That means spring will be early. If it is sunny, you will see it. That means six more weeks of winter. Just call it like you see it."

The next morning was the big day. Fred walked out of the burrow. There were a few clouds in the sky. Fred looked to his left. Then, he looked to his right. He could not see his shadow.

"Spring will be early this year," Fred said boldly. The crowd was happy. But then the clouds passed, and the sun came out. Fred saw his shadow.

"Wait," Fred said. "I mean we will have six more weeks of winter!"

The crowd started to whisper.

"There's nothing worse than a groundhog that can't make up his mind!"

Fred looked toward the burrow. Just then, Phil came out. The sky clouded over again. Phil could not see his shadow.

"Early spring," Phil said. The crowd cheered.

Activity: What do you think will happen next? On the back of this page, write an ending to the story. Make sure to begin your sentences with capital letters and end them with periods.

Name_____   Date _____

Animal Fact File

Directions: Read the fact file. Then answer the questions.

What do groundhogs look like?
- Groundhogs are brown and furry.
- Groundhogs have sharp claws and short tails.
- Groundhogs are about two feet long.
- Groundhogs weigh about 13 pounds.

What do groundhogs eat?
- Groundhogs eat grasses.
- Groundhogs eat plants.
- Groundhogs eat berries.
- Groundhogs eat insects.

Where do groundhogs live?
- Groundhogs live in burrows. A burrow can be a hole or tunnel in the ground.

How do groundhogs behave?
- Groundhogs are good diggers and climbers.
- Groundhogs hibernate in the winter.
- Groundhogs are not friendly to people.

---

1. What is a burrow?

   a. It is like a nest in a tree.   **b.** It is like a tunnel in the ground.   **c.** It is something that groundhogs eat.

2. Why do groundhogs have sharp claws?

   a. to help dig their burrows   **b.** to help eat insects   **c.** to help eat grasses

3. If you see a groundhog, what should you do?

   a. try to pet it   **b.** walk away   **c.** scream

Name_____ **Date** _____

Show What You Know

Directions: Use the Animal Fact File on page 18 to help you complete this organizer about groundhogs.

What Do They Look Like?

What Do They Eat?

GROUNDHOGS

Where Do They Live?

What Can They Do?

Name_____ Date _____

A Groundhog Is Also a Woodchuck

Did you know that another name for a groundhog is a woodchuck? There is a tongue-twister about woodchucks. A tongue-twister is something that is hard to say. Sometimes, it is hard because all the words begin with the same letter. Other times, it is hard because you have to repeat the same word over and over.

Read the woodchuck tongue-twister below. Then practice saying it until you can do it without making any mistakes!

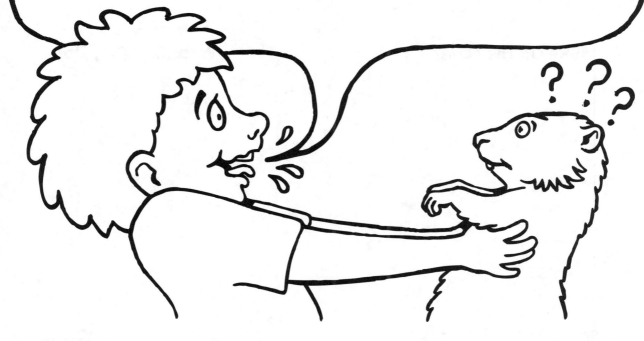

How much wood would a woodchuck chuck
If a woodchuck could chuck wood?
He would chuck, he would, as much as he could
And chuck as much as a woodchuck would
If a woodchuck could chuck wood.

Valentine's Day

February 14

Valentine's Day is all about love. On this day, we celebrate how much we love our family and our friends. On Valentine's Day, we give cards. Sometimes, we give flowers and candy. You see the color red on this day. You will see red hearts and red roses. On this day, grown-ups go out on dates. It is a fun day. It is good to show how much you love the people in your life.

Summary of Activities

Reading: Literature
Hello, Valentine!—fictional story with comprehension questions

Reading: Informational Text
The Heart—nonfiction passage with comprehension questions

Writing
I Love You This Much!—activity in which students share their feelings with loved ones

Bonus
Wearing Your Heart on Your Sleeve—graphic-organizer activity about sharing feelings

Vocabulary: love, valentine

Name_____ **Date** _____

Hello, Valentine!

Directions: Read the story. Then answer the questions on page 23.

Kim liked to walk home from school. She would walk past the corner store. She would walk past the church. She would walk past the park.

One day, as she walked past the park, she heard a strange sound. It sounded a little like a squeak. It was a soft sound. Kim did not know what it was. She had never heard a sound like it before.

When Kim got home, she asked her dad about it.

"Dad, I heard this funny sound at the park. I can't figure out what it is."

"I'll tell you what," Kim's dad said. "Let's walk past after dinner and see if we can hear it."

Kim and her dad walked down the street to the park. As soon as they got close to the fence, they heard the sound.

"Shhh," Kim's dad said.

He walked toward the little squeak. The sound was coming from under a big piece of cardboard. Kim's dad lifted it up.

"Ahhh," they both said. There was a tiny black kitten. It looked up at them.

"Meow," it squeaked.

When they got home, they put the kitten into a shoebox. They gave it a small towel to use as a blanket. They gave it some water.

"Can I keep him?" Kim asked her dad.

"Well, I guess so. But you have to take care of him. Kittens need love like babies do. And you will have to think of a good name."

All night, Kim thought and thought about what to call her tiny black kitten. The next morning, Kim came down to breakfast. She brought the shoebox with the tiny kitten inside. Her dad asked about the kitten's name.

"I can't think of a single thing," Kim said.

"Well, I have a great idea," Kim's dad said. He got a calendar.

"Put your finger on today's date," he said to Kim. So Kim put her finger on the 14. It was February 14. There was a heart on the date. Kim smiled.

"I got it!" she said. She took the lid off of the shoebox and looked inside. The kitten squeaked. Kim lifted the kitten up. "Hello, Valentine!"

Name_____ **Date** _____

Hello, Valentine! *(cont.)*

Directions: Read the story on page 22. Then answer the questions.

1. What is the name of the main character in the story?

    a. Kim   **b.** Valentine   **c.** Dad

2. Why is *Valentine* a good name for the kitten?

    a. because Kim loves the kitten
    b. because they got the kitten close to Valentine's Day
    c. because the kitten likes to eat candy

3. Where was the kitten hiding?

    a. in a shoebox   **b.** next to the church   **c.** under a piece of cardboard

Name_____   Date _____

The Heart

Directions: Read the passage. Then answer the questions.

On Valentine's Day, you will see lots of hearts that look like this. You may see hearts like this on cards. You may see hearts like this on a box of candy. But this is not what your heart really looks like. We draw hearts like this just for fun.

The Real Heart

Look at the picture to the right. This is what the heart really looks like. The heart is a muscle. It is in the middle of your chest. It is about the size of your fist.

The heart is a pump. It has a big job to do. It moves the blood throughout your body. Blood flows in and out of your heart. When you feel or hear your heart beat, you know that it is doing its job.

The Healthy Heart

You need your heart to live. You have to take care of it. You can do these things to make sure that you have a healthy heart:

- Exercise every day! To keep your heart fit, you have to make it pump hard. When you run, dance, or swim, your heart pumps fast. This makes your heart strong.
- Eat healthy food! Fruits and veggies are good to eat. Your heart likes these kinds of foods. Food that has lots of fat like chips and fries are bad for your heart.
- Smile! Your heart likes it when you feel calm and happy. There will be good times and bad times. Try not to worry. The bad times don't last forever!

1. Which one of these is best for your heart?
   a. playing video games   **b.** riding a bike   **c.** watching a movie

2. What is the heart's job?
   a. to exercise   **b.** to love   **c.** to move blood throughout the body

3. Which food is good for the heart?
   a. an apple   **b.** an ice-cream cone   **c.** French fries

Name_____ **Date** _____

I Love You This Much!

On Valentine's Day, we show how much we love the people in our lives. Think of whom you love very much. Is it your mom? Is it your cat? Is it your friend?

Write a letter to this person or pet. Tell this person or pet why you love him or her so much. Make sure to begin your sentences with capital letters and end them with periods.

Dear _____,

_____

_____

_____

_____

_____

_____

_____

Love,

_____

Name_____   **Date** _____

Wearing Your Heart on Your Sleeve

When you show how you feel to others, it is called "wearing your heart on your sleeve." That just means that people can see how you feel.

Think of four people who are very special to you. Write their names in black in each part of the heart. Color the heart red. Then cut out the heart and pin it onto your sleeve.

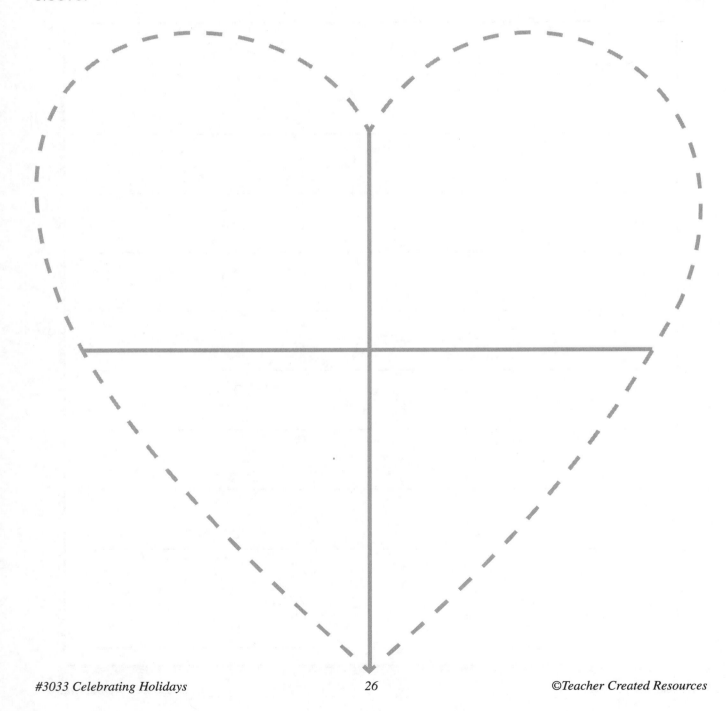

Presidents' Day

The Third Monday in February

The president is the leader of the United States. On Presidents' Day, we thank all the people who were ever president. We thank the person who is the president right now. Being president is a tough job. We have had more than 40 presidents so far. On Presidents' Day, you will see lots of red, white, and blue. These are the colors of the American flag. There is no school on Presidents' Day.

Summary of Activities

Reading: Literature
Thank You, Presidents!—poem with a writing prompt

Reading: Informational Text
Mount Rushmore—nonfiction passage with comprehension questions

Writing
If I Were President . . .—activity in which students write about what they would do if they were president

Speaking & Listening
Recite a Poem—activity in which students practice reciting "Thank You, Presidents" in front of family and friends

Vocabulary: carve, honor, memorial, president, United States of America

Thank You, Presidents!

Directions: Read the poem. Then complete the activity.

First, there was a man named George.
He fought a war at Valley Forge.
He helped the people take a stand.
He is the father of our land.

Jefferson was really wise.
He made our country twice its size.
From France, he bought a chunk of land;
From coast to coast, our nation spanned.

Lincoln was a mighty man,
When slavery had swept the land;
Because of him, the slaves were freed.
He is remembered for this deed.

Teddy Roosevelt had a plan
To set aside some wild land.
Those became our national parks,
And this is how he made his mark.

To be the president is tough.
Things can get a little rough.
So thank you, presidents—every one—
For all the things that you have done!

Activity: Do you know the name of our president? Write his or her name on the line below. On the back of this page, draw a picture of the president.

Name_____ Date _____

Mount Rushmore

Directions: Read the passage. Then answer the questions.

Below is a picture of Mount Rushmore. It is in the state of South Dakota. The faces of four presidents are carved into the side of a mountain.

Do you know any of these faces? Can you name them? The names of the presidents are:

- George Washington
- Thomas Jefferson
- Theodore Roosevelt
- Abraham Lincoln

Mount Rushmore is a memorial. That means it is something that was made to help us remember the good things that people did. Here are some facts about Mount Rushmore:

- The faces are 60 feet high.
- The noses are 20 feet long.
- The mouths are 18 feet wide.
- The eyes are 11 feet across.
- It took 14 years to carve the mountain.
- It took 400 men to carve the mountain.
- It cost about one million dollars to make.
- About three million people visit each year.

1. Where is Mount Rushmore?
   a. South Dakota　　　　**b.** Washington, D.C.　　　　**c.** New York

2. What does a memorial do?
   a. helps us to forget　　**b.** helps us to remember　　**c.** helps us to have fun

3. How long are the noses?
   a. 60 feet　　　　　　　**b.** 11 feet　　　　　　　**c.** 20 feet

Name_____ **Date** _____

If I Were President . . .

On Presidents' Day, we thank all of the presidents. It is hard to be president. Some people like what you do. Some people don't like what you do. You have to work hard. You have to be smart.

Do you think you would like to be president? What would you like to do if you were? Write three things you would do. Make sure to end each sentence with a period.

1. **If I were president, I would** _____

_____

_____

_____

2. **If I were president, I would** _____

_____

_____

_____

3. **If I were president, I would** _____

_____

_____

_____

Name_____ **Date** _____

Recite a Poem

Directions: Read the poem aloud a few times. When you think you know it, recite it for a family member or friend.

Thank You, Presidents!

First, there was a man named George.
He fought a war at Valley Forge.
He helped the people take a stand.
He is the father of our land.

Jefferson was really wise.
He made our country twice its size.
From France, he bought a chunk of land;
From coast to coast, our nation spanned.

Lincoln was a mighty man,
When slavery had swept the land;
Because of him the slaves were freed.
He is remembered for this deed.

Teddy Roosevelt had a plan
To set aside some wild land.
Those became our national parks,
And this is how he made his mark.

To be the president is tough.
Things can get a little rough.
So thank you, presidents—every one—
For all the things that you have done!

Chinese New Year

The First Day of the Chinese Calendar—Late January or Early February

Pop! Bang! Do you hear that? Those are firecrackers! It must be Chinese New Year! This is a time to say hello to a brand-new year. At this time, people clean their homes and buy new clothes. You may see a dancing dragon, and you may hear loud drums. You might even get some money in a red packet! It is a time for family, friends, and fun!

Summary of Activities

Reading: Literature
How the Years Got Their Names—fictional story with a sequencing activity

Reading: Informational Text
How Do You Eat?—nonfiction passage with comprehension questions

Writing
Are You Lucky?—activity in which students write about a time when they were lucky

Bonus
The Red Packet—activity in which students make red packets and fill them with an even amount of money

Vocabulary: China, Chinese, chopsticks, culture, dragon, firecracker, luck(y)

Name_____   Date _____

How the Years Got Their Names

Directions: Read the story. Then complete the activity on page 34.

This story is set in China. Once there were 12 animals. There was a dog, a rat, an ox, a tiger, a rabbit, a rooster, a snake, a ram, a dragon, a horse, a pig, and a monkey. They lived by a big river.

One day, the animals had a fight. They wanted each year to have a name.

"I think this year should be named after me," the dog said.

"No," said the pig. "I think it should be named after me."

"No," said the snake. "I think it should be named after me."

The gods heard the fight.

"Stop fighting," they said. "We will have a race. Do you see the big river? We will name this year after the one who can get across the river first."

The animals lined up on one side of the river. On the count of three, they all jumped in!

The ox was strong. He swam fast. Soon, he was in the lead. But the rat was smart. He grabbed the ox's tail and climbed onto his back. The ox did not know the rat was there!

The ox thought he was going to win the race. Just before the ox got to the other side, the rat jumped off. He landed in the grass. The rat won the race!

The ox laughed. "How did you do that?" he asked.

The gods thought it was funny, too. "The rat is the winner," they said. "This year is the Year of the Rat. The ox was second. Next year will be the Year of the Ox."

The other animals finished the race. This is the order they came in: The tiger was third. The rabbit was fourth. The dragon was fifth. The snake was sixth. The horse was seventh. The ram was eighth. The monkey was ninth. The rooster was tenth. The dog was eleventh. The pig was last.

This is how the years on the Chinese calendar got their names.

Name_____   Date _____

How the Years Got Their Names (cont.)

Directions: Read the story on page 33. Write the names of the animals on the lines. Then put a number 1 through 12 in the box to show the order the animals finished the race.

Name_____   Date _____

How Do You Eat?

Directions: Read the passage. Then answer the questions.

There are some foods that you can eat with your hands. You can eat pizza with your hands. You can eat a hot dog with your hands. These foods are called "finger foods." But most of the time, you eat using a fork. People have been eating with forks for a long time.

A fork has a handle. A fork usually has four prongs. You hold a fork with your fingers. A fork is a tool. It helps you pick up food and put it into your mouth.

In some places, people do not use forks to eat. In China, they use chopsticks. Chopsticks are a pair of sticks. The sticks are the same length. The sticks are skinnier at one end. Most of the time, chopsticks are made of wood.

Chopsticks are like forks. They are a tool. They help you pick up food and put it into your mouth. You hold chopsticks with your fingers. People have been eating with chopsticks for a long time.

Chopstick Rules

Here are some things to remember if you eat with chopsticks:

- Do not tap your chopsticks on your bowl.
- Do not spear your food with your chopsticks.
- Do not use your chopsticks upside down.
- Do place your chopsticks on the top of your bowl when you are finished eating.

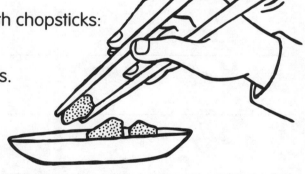

1. Which one is a "finger food"?
   a. banana   **b.** soup   **c.** pasta

2. Chopsticks are
   a. a toy.   **b.** a tool.   **c.** a finger food.

3. What should you **not** do with your chopsticks?
   a. eat with them   **b.** tap your bowl   **c.** place them on the top of your bowl

Name_____ **Date** _____

Are You Lucky?

During Chinese New Year, we wish for good luck for the coming year. Have you ever been lucky? In the space below, tell about a time when you had good luck. Make sure to begin your sentences with capital letters and end them with periods.

_____

_____

_____

_____

_____

_____

_____

_____

_____

_____

Name_____   Date _____

The Red Packet

If it is Chinese New Year, you may get a bright-red packet! Inside, there will be some money. You may get two dollars. You may get eight dollars. There will always be an even amount of money inside.

Now, it is time to make your lucky red packet. You will need:

- red copy paper
- green copy paper
- scissors
- glue

Follow **these** directions:

1. Copy the outline of the red packet (page 38) onto the red paper. (teacher step)

2. Cut out the packet along the dashed lines.

3. Fold it along the solid lines. Fold away from the Chinese characters.

4. Lay the packet flat, and smooth it out.

5. Glue two of the sides closed.

6. Copy the money (below) onto the green paper. (teacher step)

7. Cut out the money to put in the red packet. Make sure that you only put an even amount of money in the packet.

Name_____ **Date** _____

The Red Packet *(cont.)*

St. Patrick's Day

March 17

On St. Patrick's Day, everyone is Irish! On this day, we celebrate Irish culture. St. Patrick was a priest in Ireland who lived long ago. It is said that he drove all of the snakes out of Ireland. On St. Patrick's Day, you will see parades. You will see people wearing green. You will see four-leaf clovers.

Summary of Activities

Reading: Literature
How to Spot a Leprechaun—fictional story with a drawing activity

Reading: Informational Text
One Potato, Two Potato—recipe with comprehension questions

Writing
Three Wishes—activity in which students write about what they would wish for if they had three wishes

Speaking & Listening
Irish Folk Music and Instruments—activity in which students learn about and listen to some musical instruments that are used in Irish folk music

Vocabulary: clover, culture, Ireland, Irish, leprechaun, parade, potato

Name_____ **Date** _____

How to Spot a Leprechaun

Directions: Read the story. Then complete the activity.

   Would you like to meet a leprechaun? First, you have to find one. Here are some facts about leprechauns that may help. But be careful! Leprechauns like to play tricks on people.

Leprechaun Facts

- Leprechauns are fairies.
- They are old men with beards.
- They are about two feet tall.
- Their job is to make shoes.
- They have pots of gold coins.
- They hide their pots of gold at the ends of rainbows.
- They can be grumpy.
- They wear hats and green clothes.
- They wear shoes with buckles.
- They live in the woods.
- They can do magic.

Activity: Use the facts above to draw a picture of a leprechaun. Make sure your picture shows where he lives. Show the leprechaun doing his work.

Name_____ Date _____

One Potato, Two Potato

Directions: Read the recipe. Then answer the questions.

On St. Patrick's Day, people like to eat Irish potatoes. They are not real potatoes. They are a kind of cookie. They are sweet and tasty. They are easy to make. Why not try to make some Irish potatoes this St. Patrick's Day? Follow the recipe below.

What You Will Need

- 1 cup powdered sugar
- 1 cup shredded coconut
- $1\frac{1}{2}$ tablespoons cream
- 2 tablespoons ground cinnamon
- plastic bag

What You Will Do

① Mix the sugar with the coconut.

② Add the cream and stir until it makes a dough.

③ Put the cinnamon in a plastic bag.

④ Roll the dough into small balls.

⑤ Put the balls in the bag and shake gently.

⑥ Share with friends!

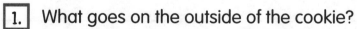

1. What goes on the outside of the cookie?
   a. cinnamon   **b.** sugar   **c.** coconut

2. What do you do second?
   a. Roll the dough into balls.   **b.** Add the cream and stir.   **c.** Put the balls in the bag.

3. What shape are the cookies?
   a. square   **b.** flat   **c.** round

Name_____ **Date** _____

Three Wishes

It is hard to catch a leprechaun. They are smart. They know that people try to catch them to steal their pots of gold. If you do catch a leprechaun, he will grant you three wishes.

If you had a chance to make three wishes come true, what would they be? Write your three wishes. Make sure to end your sentences with periods.

1. **I would wish for** _____

_____

_____

_____

2. **I would wish for** _____

_____

_____

_____

3. **I would wish for** _____

_____

_____

_____

Name_____   Date _____

Irish Folk Music and Instruments

Music is a big part of St. Patrick's Day. On this day, people listen to Irish folk music. Go to the link below to hear what some of the instruments used in this kind of music sound like.

www.allmusic.com/style/irish-folk-ma0000002666

Earth Day

April 22

Earth is our home. We have to care for it. On April 22, we show how much we love and care for our home. On Earth Day, we learn new ways to keep Earth clean. On Earth Day, we share ways to help protect Earth.

Summary of Activities

Reading: Literature
M and M's Bat House—fictional story with a drawing activity

Reading: Informational Text
Great Things About Earth—nonfiction passage with a coloring activity

Writing
Why I Love Earth—activity in which students write about what they love about Earth

Speaking & Listening
My Favorite Place—activity in which students describe their favorite places

Vocabulary: build, Earth, oceans, protect

Name_____ Date _____

M and M's Bat House

Directions: Read the story. Then complete the activity.

Meg was thinking of a project she could do on Earth Day. Some kids planned to plant trees. Others were going to collect trash. I want to do something different, she thought. She asked her older brother, Mike.

"I have a great idea," he said. "I think you should build a bat house!"

"Yuck, no way," Meg said. "Bats are scary."

"Bats are cool," Mike said. "And they have a job to do."

Mike told Meg all about bats. "Bats eat tons of bugs," Mike said. "If it weren't for them, we would be covered in bug bites!"

Mike also told Meg how the bats help the flowers just like the bees.

"I don't see what bats have to do with Earth Day," Meg said.

"Earth Day is about helping Earth and everything that needs her, like the bats! Sometimes they live in caves, but they also live in trees."

Mike looked around. "Do you see any trees around here?" he asked Meg.

Meg and Mike got to work. Mike looked online to get some ideas. They got wood, some paint, and a hammer and nails. They had their bat house done in no time at all.

"We have to do one more thing," Meg said.

She picked up a paintbrush and some paint. On the front of the bat house she wrote, "M and M's Bat House. All Bats Welcome!"

"Now all we need to do is find a good place for it," Meg said. "It needs to be in the sun, high off the ground, and near water."

Meg and Mike lived in a big city in a row house. There were not very many trees, but the roofs of the houses were perfect. They were high off the ground and in the sun.

Meg and Mike asked their dad if he could put the bat house out on the roof.

"Sure," he said. "And I have a great idea. I will put a big bowl out there, too, that will catch all the rainwater. This way, the bats won't get thirsty."

"The bat house is the best Earth Day project ever," Meg said.

"Yup," said Mike. "We help the bats, the bats help Earth, and Earth helps us!"

Activity: On the back of this page, draw a picture of the bat house built by Meg and Mike.

Name_____ **Date** _____

Great Things About Earth

Directions: Read the passage. Then complete the activity.

Earth is our home. There are lots of great things about Earth. Here is a list of some of them:

① Earth is green. It is covered in trees, plants, grasses, and flowers.

② Earth is blue. It is mostly covered in deep, blue oceans.

③ Earth has all kinds of animals. It has birds that fly up high and fish that swim down low. Earth has lions that roar and mice that squeak.

④ Earth has a sky with a sun, a moon, and stars.

⑤ Earth has mountains covered in snow and beaches covered in sand.

⑥ Earth has spring, summer, fall, and winter.

⑦ Earth has thunder, lightning, wind, and rain.

⑧ Earth makes the air, the water, and the food we need to live.

⑨ Earth has all the people in the world.

⑩ Earth has our family and our friends.

Activity: Look at the picture of Earth. Color the water blue and the land green.

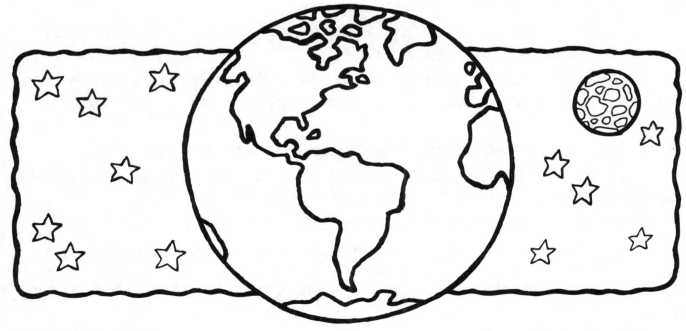

Name_____ **Date** _____

Why I Love Earth

Earth is our home. It is the only home we will ever have. We share Earth with everyone else. We all have to love and care for it.

In the space below, make a list of three things that you love about Earth. Make sure to end your sentences with periods.

1. **I love Earth because** _____

   _____

   _____

   _____

2. **I love Earth because** _____

   _____

   _____

   _____

3. **I love Earth because** _____

   _____

   _____

   _____

Name_____   **Date** _____

My Favorite Place

What is your favorite place? Is it your house? Is it the beach? Is it a park? Describe your favorite place on Earth. Make sure to tell what it looks like. Explain why you love it so much. Then share your response with a classmate.

_____

_____

_____

_____

_____

_____

_____

_____

_____

_____

Cinco de Mayo

May 5

Cinco de Mayo is how you say "May 5" in Spanish. This is the day that we celebrate the culture of Mexico. It is an important day for Mexicans. On this day, you will hear Mexican music, break a piñata, and maybe eat some yummy food like tacos and burritos!

Summary of Activities

Reading: Literature
The Piñata—fictional story with comprehension questions and a drawing activity

Reading: Informational Text
Tacos—nonfiction passage with a food-related activity

Writing
Tacos for Two—activity in which students write about making tacos for friends

Speaking & Listening
The Piñata Song—activity in which students learn how to sing a song in Spanish and English

Vocabulary: burrito, culture, Mexicans, Mexico, piñata, Spain, Spanish, taco

Name_____ Date _____

The Piñata

Directions: Read the story. Then answer the questions and complete the activity on page 51.

John felt great. He was going to his first Cinco de Mayo party. His friend, Juan, asked him to come. Juan's family was from Mexico.

When John told his mom, she said, "Cinco de Mayo? Watch out for the piñata!"

"Pin what?" John asked.

His mom laughed. "You'll find out."

John did not know what a piñata was. He asked his sister.

"Ruth, what is a piñata?"

"You don't know?" she asked.

"No, but I am going to Juan's party. There will be one there."

"Well, I guess you will find out then."

John thought about the piñata all day. He couldn't wait to find out what it was.

When John got to the party, he looked around. He saw a table full of food. It smelled great. He heard loud music. It sounded fun. But he didn't see a thing that could be a piñata. Then he saw his friend, Juan.

"Come outside," Juan said. "We are going to break the piñata!"

John ran outside with his friend. He saw the piñata hanging from a tree. It was a big star made of paper. It was pink, white, and blue.

"Grab the stick," Juan said.

John picked up the stick from the ground. Each child had a turn to hit and poke the piñata. The adults stood around them and sang a song. It was John's turn.

"Hit it hard," Juan said.

John hit as hard as he could. All of a sudden, the piñata burst open! *Oh, no,* John thought. *I broke it.* But everyone cheered! Candy and small toys fell out of the piñata. The kids ran to pick them up.

"Wow," John said. "Now I know what a piñata is! I can't wait for Cinco de Mayo next year!"

Name_____ Date _____

The Piñata *(cont.)*

Directions: Read the story on page 50. Then answer the questions. Complete the activity below.

1. What is the setting of the story?
   a. school   **b.** a park   **c.** a party

2. Who is the main character in the story?
   a. John   **b.** Juan   **c.** Ruth

3. What is the stick used for?
   a. to make a fire   **b.** to break the piñata   **c.** to play a game

Activity: Draw a picture of John breaking the piñata.

Name_____ **Date** _____

Tacos

Directions: Read the passage. Then complete the activity.

One of the best things about Cinco de Mayo is the food. Mexican food is good to eat. Tacos are a kind of Mexican food. Lots of people love tacos. They are tasty.

A taco is made with a tortilla. This is a soft piece of bread. It is round like a circle. You can put things that you like to eat inside of it. Then you fold it in half.

Activity: Look at the food below. Draw a circle around the things you would like to put in your taco.

Name_____ **Date** _____

Tacos for Two

In the space below, write about how you would make a taco for yourself and for your best friend. What would you put in your taco? What would you put in your best friend's taco? Make sure to begin your sentences with capital letters and end them with periods.

Your Taco

_____

_____

_____

_____

Your Best Friend's Taco

_____

_____

_____

_____

Name_____ **Date** _____

The Piñata Song

Would you like to learn the song that the grown-ups were singing when John broke the piñata? Here it is below. Try to learn it in Spanish and English.

Spanish

Dale, dale, dale.
No pierdas el tino.
Porque si lo pierdes,
Pierdes el camino.
Ya le diste una.
Ya le diste dos.
Ya le diste tres.
Y tu tiempo se acabo.

English

Hit it, hit it, hit it.
Don't lose your aim.
Because if you lose it,
You lose the way.
You hit it once.
You hit it twice.
You hit it three times.
And your time is up.

Mother's Day

The Second Sunday in May

Happy Mother's Day! This is the day that we thank moms for all of the things they do. Being a mom is a big job. Moms do so much. Maybe your mom cooks your dinner. Maybe your mom helps you with your homework. Maybe your mom drives you to school. Moms care for us when we are sick or sad. Moms even love us when we do wrong. Moms do all these things and so much more! On Mother's Day, it is good to do something nice for moms.

Summary of Activities

Reading: Literature
Happy Mother's Day—a poem with a drawing activity

Reading: Informational Text
A Gift for Mom—nonfiction passage with comprehension questions

Writing
My Mom—activity in which students write about what they love about their moms

Speaking & Listening
Name Those Moms—activity in which students play a game of Telephone using the names of their mothers

Vocabulary: brunch, grandmom, mom, mother

Name_____ **Date** _____

Happy Mother's Day

Directions: Read the poem. Then complete the activity.

There is a person like no other.

She is a gem we call a mother.

A mother's job is never done.

She's up most days before the sun

And doesn't rest until after dark.

We love our moms with all our heart.

When we are sick, our mother's there,

She gives us lots of tender care,

And if we're scared to shut the light,

Our moms will hold us very tight.

If we feel sad and want to cry,

Our moms are there to dry our eyes.

And when we have a spelling test,

Our moms will help us do our best.

She cooks us breakfast, lunch, and dinner.

I have to say that moms are winners.

So thanks for everything you do.

We hope you know we love you, too.

So there's really nothing left to say,

But happy, happy Mother's Day!

Activity: On the back of the page, draw a picture of a mom.

56

Name_____   Date _____

A Gift for Mom

Directions: Read the passage. Then answer the questions.

Mother's Day is the day that we say thank you to our moms. We can also say thank you to our grandmoms. They take care of us, too!

There are lots of ways to say thank you. Some people like to buy their moms a gift. You will have to choose a gift that you think your mom will like.

Some moms like to get flowers. Some moms like to get pretty cards. Some moms like to go out for brunch. Brunch is a meal that you eat at about 11:00. It is between breakfast and lunch.

You don't have to buy your mom a gift. You don't have to take her to brunch. You could do something nice for her instead.

One thing that you could do is to clean up your room. Put all of your clothes away. Make your bed. Moms really like when they get help around the house!

You could take a picture of yourself and give it to your mom. Moms love to have photos of their children.

The best thing you could do for your mom is to tell her how much you love her! You could thank her for all the things that she does for you.

Don't forget to give your mom a big hug and kiss. She will like that the best of all!

---

1. What do some moms like to get on Mother's Day?
   a. flowers   **b.** dogs   **c.** ice cream

2. What is brunch?
   a. the same as dinner   **b.** the same as breakfast   **c.** a meal between breakfast and lunch

3. What could you do on Mother's Day?
   a. watch TV   **b.** clean your room   **c.** take a nap

Name_____ **Date** _____

My Mom

Think about what you love about your mom. Pick the top three things, and write them in the spaces below. Make sure to end your sentences with periods.

1. **I love my mom because** _____

_____

_____

_____

2. **I love my mom because** _____

_____

_____

_____

3. **I love my mom because** _____

_____

_____

_____

Name_____ **Date** _____

Name Those Moms

This is a variation of the game Telephone. Explain to students that they are going to have to be very good listeners to play this game. Ask a student to say the first name of his or her mom or the person who takes care of them. Ask a second student to repeat the first mom's name and then say his or her mother's name. Move on to a third student and repeat until all students have had a turn.

Memorial Day

The Last Monday in May

On Memorial Day, we remember soldiers who died serving our country. Soldiers keep us safe. They protect us. We honor them on this day. There is no school on Memorial Day. Many people do not go to work on Memorial Day. It is a day to remember.

Summary of Activities

Reading: Literature
The Picnic—fictional story with comprehension questions

Reading: Informational Text
Flag Facts—nonfiction passage with a writing activity

Writing
Summer Begins!—activity in which students tell about what they like to do during the summertime

Speaking & Listening
Tell a Memorial Day Story—activity in which students tell a story based on a picture

Vocabulary: grave, honor, memorial, remember, soldier, summertime, uniform, war

Name_____ Date _____

The Picnic

Directions: Read the story. Then answer the questions on page 62.

Kate woke up early on Memorial Day. She was going to a picnic. She put her swimsuit and towel in a bag. Then she went to the kitchen to help her mom. Kate helped her mom pack the lunch. They put cheese and fruit into a basket.

"I think we are ready," Kate's mom said.

It was a warm day. When they got to the picnic, some kids were in the pool. Kate saw some grown-ups dressed in strange clothes.

"What are they wearing?" she asked her mom.

"They are soldiers," Kate's mom said. "They are wearing uniforms. Our country is free. We can live as we like. We can say what we like. You have to fight for those things. The soldiers fight for us. But some die doing it."

Kate looked at the soldiers. They looked scary to her.

"Do they always dress like that?" she asked.

"No. But today is Memorial Day. It's the day that we remember the soldiers who lost their lives."

Kate looked sad. "I thought it was the start of summer," she said.

Her mom smiled. "It is that, too. It's O.K. to have some fun. But it is also good to remember."

Kate asked her mom how you remember.

"You can put a flag on a soldier's grave. You can put some flowers there. Most of all, you can remember that some soldiers fought wars and gave their lives so that we could live free."

Kate looked at the soldiers again. This time, she wasn't scared.

Name_____   **Date** _____

The Picnic *(cont.)*

Directions: Read the story on page 61. Then answer the questions.

1. Where do you think the story is set?
   - **a.** in a school
   - **b.** in a church
   - **c.** in a park

2. Who is the main character of the story?
   - **a.** a soldier
   - **b.** Kate's mom
   - **c.** Kate

3. What should we do on Memorial Day?
   - **a.** go on a picnic
   - **b.** remember soldiers who died
   - **c.** go swimming

Name_____   **Date** _____

Flag Facts

Directions: Read the passage. Then complete the activity.

On Memorial Day, you will see lots of American flags. People put small flags on the graves of soldiers. People put flags in front of their houses. This is a way to honor soldiers who have died. Here are some facts about our flag:

- Our flag is red, white, and blue.

- Our flag has 7 red stripes.

- A red stripe is always at the top and the bottom.

- Our flag has 6 white stripes.

- Our flag has 50 white stars.

- The white stars are on a blue rectangle.

- Each white star has 5 points.

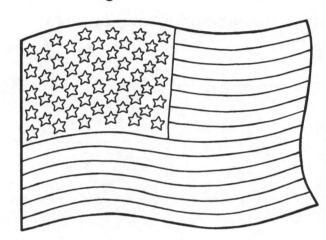

Activity: Write two sentences about the American flag. Make sure to end your sentences with periods.

1. **Our flag** _____

   _____

   _____

2. **Our flag** _____

   _____

   _____

Name_____   **Date** _____

Summer Begins!

Memorial Day marks the beginning of summertime! In the space below, write three things that you love to do during the summer months. Make sure to end your sentences with periods.

1. **In the summertime, I love to** _____

_____

_____

_____

2. **In the summertime, I love to** _____

_____

_____

_____

3. **In the summertime, I love to** _____

_____

_____

_____

Name_____ Date _____

Tell a Memorial Day Story

Directions: Look at the picture below. Tell someone a story about what is happening in the picture. Answer these questions:

- Who is in this picture?
- Where are they?
- What are they doing?
- Why is this important?

Father's Day

Third Sunday in June

Happy Father's Day! On this day, we thank dads for all that they do for us. We tell our dads how much we love them. We can buy our dads gifts. We can take our dads out to do something fun.

Summary of Activities

Reading: Literature
The Best Dad Ever!—fictional story with comprehension questions

Reading: Informational Text
The Necktie—nonfiction passage about neckties with a drawing activity

Writing
My Dad—activity in which students write about what they love about their dads

Speaking & Listening
Dad Tales—activity in which students tell stories about their dads

Vocabulary: dad, father, hatched, necktie

Name_____   Date _____

The Best Dad Ever!

Directions: Read the story. Then answer the questions.

My dad is the best! Even before I was born, he was great.

My mom told me the whole story. She said that once I was growing inside of an egg. I was inside of my egg for a long time.

When I was in my egg, my mom had to go to work. Her job was to swim out to sea. She had to get food for our family. She was gone for two whole months!

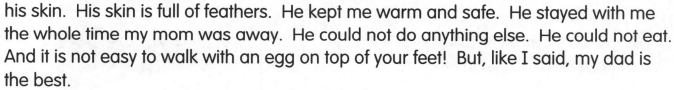

While she was away, my dad took care of me. He put my egg on top of his feet. He covered my egg with his skin. His skin is full of feathers. He kept me warm and safe. He stayed with me the whole time my mom was away. He could not do anything else. He could not eat. And it is not easy to walk with an egg on top of your feet! But, like I said, my dad is the best.

When my mom came home, I **hatched**. I came out of my egg. I saw my mom and my dad for the first time! My mom fed me. Then it was my dad's turn to go to work.

The next year, my dad had another egg on top of his feet. It was my brother. He did the same thing with him as he did with me.

We both love our dad very much. We are here because of him. When we grow up, we will do the same for our children. We will put the eggs on top of our feet. We will keep the eggs safe and warm. We will be great dads, too!

1. Who is telling the story?
   a. a little boy   **b.** a penguin   **c.** an egg

2. What does the word *hatched* mean?
   a. to come out of an egg   **b.** to break   **c.** to be a good dad

3. Where does the dad put the egg?
   a. on top of his head   **b.** under his wing   **c.** on top of his feet

Name_____ **Date** _____

The Necktie

Directions: Read the passage. Then complete the activity.

Lots of dads wear neckties. You can give your dad a necktie on Father's Day.

Most neckties are made from a piece of cloth. They are worn around the neck. They are worn with a shirt that has a collar. A necktie has a knot. They are mostly worn by men. Here are some types of neckties. Which one do you like the best?

Long ties can come in many colors and patterns. One of these long ties has stripes. The other is covered in polka dots.

The tie on the right is called a bow tie. It is worn on special occasions.

Take a look at the bolo tie. This tie is made from a long piece of cord. Does the bolo tie make you think of a cowboy?

There are some ties that you don't need to tie at all. They are called clip-on ties. A clip-on tie has a metal clip on the back. You can clip it to the collar of your shirt.

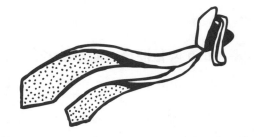

Activity: On the back of this page, draw a picture of you and your dad wearing matching ties.

Name_____ **Date** _____

My Dad

Think about what you love about your dad. Pick the top three things, and write them in the spaces below. Make sure to end your sentences with periods.

1. **I love my dad because** _____

_____

_____

_____

2. **I love my dad because** _____

_____

_____

_____

3. **I love my dad because** _____

_____

_____

_____

Name_____ **Date** _____

Dad Tales

What is the most fun you have ever had with your dad? Share a story about a really great time that you had with him.

Ramadan

About 4 Weeks Long, Dates Change
Every Year Based on Islamic Calendar

Ramadan is a holy month for people who practice the religion of Islam. It is a time for Muslims to think about how to be better and how to help others. During this month, Muslims fast from sunrise to sunset. Ramadan ends with a big celebration called Eid-al-Fitr.

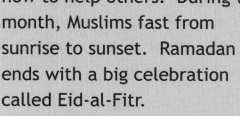

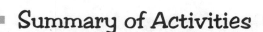

Summary of Activities

Reading: Literature
Hodja Tales—Islamic fables with a drawing activity

Reading: Informational Text
Fruit of the Palm Tree—nonfiction passage with comprehension questions

Writing
Being the Best I Can Be—activity in which students write about helping others

Bonus
Under a Crescent Moon—activity in which students make crescent-moon mosaics

Vocabulary: crescent (moon), fast, Islam, Muslim, pray, religion

Name_____ Date _____

Hodja Tales

Directions: Read the stories from Islam about a man named Hodja. Then complete the activity.

Tale #1—Duck Soup

Hodja saw a group of ducks in the lake. He tried to catch one, but he couldn't. The ducks were too fast for him. He sat by the lake. He took a loaf of bread from his sack. He broke the bread into pieces. He dunked them into the lake. Then he ate them. A man walked by and saw Hodja. He asked him what he was eating. Hodja dunked another piece of bread into the lake and said, "Duck soup."

Tale #2—Who Needs the Soap More?

Hodja and his wife took their dirty clothes to the river so they could wash them. His wife brought a bar of soap with her. She put the soap on top of the dirty clothes. While she filled a bucket with water from the river, a crow swooped down and grabbed the soap. He flew away with it. She yelled to Hodja.

"Run, Hodja! A crow just stole our soap!"

Hodja saw the crow flying away and said, "Let him have it. He needs it more than we do!"

Tale #3—Why Did He Ride the Donkey Backwards?

One day, Hodja was going to the mosque with his friends. He was riding his donkey backwards. His friends asked why he was doing that.

"Isn't it strange to ride your donkey like that?" they asked.

Hodja answered, "If I sat facing forward, then you would be behind me. If you were in front of me, then I would be behind you. If I ride my donkey this way, we can face each other."

Activity: On the back of this page, draw a picture to go along with one of the tales.

72

Name_____ Date _____

Fruit of the Palm Tree

Directions: Read the passage. Then answer the questions.

During Ramadan, Muslims do not eat any food from morning until night. This is called a *fast*. They also pray. They believe that this helps them to be closer to Allah, or God.

One of the first foods that Muslims eat at night is called the *date*. Dates are a fruit. They come from date palm trees. People have been eating dates for thousands of years.

Dates are small. They are dried like raisins. Some dates have pits in the middle. You can also get dates that do not have pits.

Dates are brown and sweet. Dates taste great, and they are also very good for you.

How to Eat Dates

There are lots of ways to eat dates. You can eat them just as a snack. You can cook things with dates. Some people make cookies and cakes with dates. You can make ice cream with dates, too. You can dip dates into honey. You can even make a peanut butter and date sandwich! Here's how:

① Toast two slices of bread.

② Spread peanut butter on the bread.

③ Chop up some pitted dates.

④ Sprinkle them onto the peanut butter.

⑤ Close the sandwich and cut it in half. Enjoy!

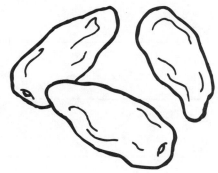

1. **What is a date?**
   a. a fruit   **b.** a tree   **c.** a raisin

2. **What is inside of some dates?**
   a. candy   **b.** a pit   **c.** peanut butter

3. **What do dates look like?**
   a. They are green.   **b.** They are big.   **c.** They are brown.

Name_____   **Date** _____

Being the Best I Can Be

During the month of Ramadan, Muslims think about how they can be better people. Now, it's your turn. In the spaces below, write three things that you could do to help others. Make sure to end your sentences with periods.

1. **I could help others by** _____

_____

_____

_____

2. **I could help others by** _____

_____

_____

_____

3. **I could help others by** _____

_____

_____

_____

Name_____ **Date** _____

Under a Crescent Moon

   A *mosaic* is a picture or pattern made from lots of tiny, different shapes. Mosaics are a part of the art of Islam.

   The month of Ramadan begins with a new crescent moon like the one pictured below.

   Cut out small squares from different colored paper. Paste the pieces onto the crescent moon to make a mosaic in honor of Ramadan.

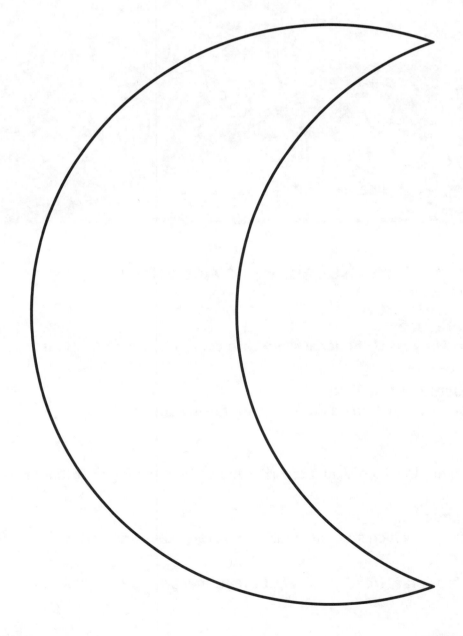

Independence Day

July 4

Happy Birthday, America! July 4 is the day that we celebrate our independence from Great Britain. On this day, we have cookouts, watch fireworks, and sing patriotic songs. There are parades and lots of red, white, and blue!

Summary of Activities

Reading: Literature
Going to See the Fireworks!—fictional story with comprehension questions

Reading: Informational Text
All-American Foods—nonfiction passage with a drawing activity

Writing
Free People—activity in which students write about the meaning of freedom

Speaking & Listening
Magic Flag—activity in which students make up a story as a whole class

Vocabulary: fireworks, freedom, Great Britain, independence, revolution

Name_____ Date _____

Going to See the Fireworks!

Directions: Read the story. Then answer the questions.

It's the Fourth of July. I am going to see the fireworks! I am going with my family. I love fireworks! I love them so much that my dad calls me "Sparkle."

Every July 4, we go to see the fireworks. They are at my church. Lots of people from my town go, too. I go with my mom, my dad, and my brother, Jim.

We take lawn chairs. We take a big blanket. We also take lots of bug spray. We don't want to spend the whole time itching.

We walk over to the church grounds an hour before the show.

"We have to get a good spot," my dad says.

But every spot is good. All you have to do to see the fireworks is look up at the sky.

My mom spreads out the blanket. My dad opens up the lawn chairs. We get ready for the big show. But it has to get dark first. We all wait in the dark.

Boom! Boom! Boom! Boom!

The fireworks start! They light up the dark. Red, white, and blue sparks shoot out into the black sky. People say "ooh" and "ahh" when they see the bright sparks!

The fireworks are loud. Sometimes, you have to put your hands over your ears. The fireworks are bright. They turn night into day for just a second.

---

1. Who is telling this story?
   a. Jim   **b.** "Sparkle"   **c.** Mom

2. Where are the fireworks?
   a. at the church grounds   **b.** at the school grounds   **c.** at the baseball field

3. What are the fireworks like?
   a. cold   **b.** hot   **c.** loud

Name_____ **Date** _____

All-American Foods

Directions: Read the passage. Then complete the activity.

Happy Birthday, U.S.A.! It's time to try some foods from where we live. Take a look at the list of sweet American treats below. How many have you tried?

Root-Beer Float

Just say "yum"! A root-beer float is so good. Just mix some vanilla ice cream with some root-beer soda in a glass. What is there not to like?

Snow Cone

A snow cone is just right for a hot summer day. It is made with shaved ice. It is covered in sweet syrup. Eat it fast, or it may melt!

Banana Split

Yes, please! This is made with one banana cut in half. Add three scoops of ice cream. Squeeze on some chocolate sauce. Cover with whipped cream. Don't forget the cherry!

Apple Pie

Apple pie is the best! It is made with sweet cooked apples. They are baked inside of a buttery pie crust. This pie is great with a scoop of ice cream. Serve it warm!

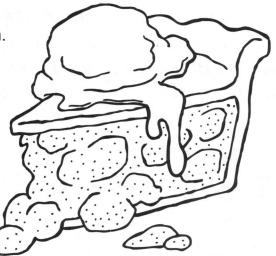

Activity: Circle the name of the food that you like best. On the back of the page, draw a picture of your favorite sweet treat.

Name_____   Date _____

Free People

On Independence Day, we think about what it means to be free. We can work where we want to work. We can go to school where we want to go to school. It is our right to live as we want to live. It is not like this everywhere.

What does freedom mean to you? Complete the sentences below. Make sure to end them with periods.

1. **Being free means** _____

_____

_____

_____

2. **Being free means** _____

_____

_____

_____

3. **Being free means** _____

_____

_____

_____

Name_____   Date _____

Magic Flag

In this teacher-directed activity, students create a story as a whole class. Here's how:

1. Bring a small American flag to class. It will be passed from one student to the next.

2. Explain to students that the American flag that you are holding is no ordinary flag. Tell them that it is magic because whoever holds it can tell great stories.

3. Explain that no one is permitted to talk unless that person is holding the flag.

4. Begin a story by making one up yourself that takes place on Independence Day.

5. When you are finished with your story starter, pass the flag to another student who will continue the story for a few more sentences.

6. When that student has finished his or her part of the story, ask him or her to pass the flag to another student.

7. Continue this way until a student decides to complete the story. Alternatively, if you want the story to be completed, indicate to students in a prearranged way. Perhaps at the beginning you all agree on a sign that will mean "wrap it up."

Labor Day

First Monday in September

Most grown-ups have a job. They have to work hard. They work almost every day. Labor Day is the day that we say thanks for all the hard work that people do. On Labor Day, most people do not have to go to work. They have a day off!

Summary of Activities

Reading: Literature
Take-Your-Child-to-Work Day—fictional story with a drawing activity

Reading: Informational Text
Jobs You See Every Day—nonfiction passage with a matching activity

Writing
When I Grow up, I Want to Be . . .—activity in which students write about what they want to be when they grow up

Speaking & Listening
Job Interview—activity in which students interview members of the school staff about their jobs

Vocabulary: job, labor, work

Name_____   Date _____

Take-Your-Child-to-Work Day

Directions: Read the story. Then complete the activity.

Kim was happy. Today, she would go with her mom to work. Kim knew what her mom did for a job. But Kim had never gone to work with her.

Kim and her mom got into the car. They drove to her office. It was in a place that used to be a house. It was big.

They went inside of the office. It didn't smell so great. Kim put her hand up to her nose. Her mom laughed. Next, her mom put on a long white coat. They went into another room.

There were some people in there who worked with Kim's mom. They all wore the same thing. They wore a light blue shirt and light blue pants. The pants were the kind that had a drawstring at the top.

Kim looked at the shelves. They were full of all kinds of bottles with pills. There were also needles on the shelves. There were two scales in the room. They looked like tables.

"I am going to feed everyone," someone said.

"Great," Kim's mom said. "And you can send in whoever is first."

Kim's mom picked up a file. She began to read it.

"Are you ready?" Kim's mom asked.

Kim nodded her head yes. Outside of the door, she heard a loud crash. Then she heard a howl, a bark, and someone say, "No, Bobo, no!"

Kim and her mom laughed. Then they opened the door.

Activity: What kind of a job does Kim's mom have? Look for clues in the story. On the back of the page, draw a picture of Kim with her mom at work.

Name_____ Date _____

Jobs You See Every Day

Directions: Read the passage. Then complete the activity on page 84.

You spend a lot of time at school. You see grown-ups all day long—and not just your teacher. All of those grown-ups are at work. They have jobs to do.

Think of all the grown-ups you see at school every day. Do you know the work that they do?

Some work in the office. They answer the phone. They sort the mail. They call your mom or dad if you have to leave school before it is time to go home. A person who does this job is called a <u>secretary</u>.

Do you take the bus to school? If you do, then you see this person all the time. The person who drives the bus is called a <u>bus driver</u>.

Do you walk to school? Then you might see someone who makes sure that you get across the street safely. This person is called a <u>crossing guard</u>.

There are people who help out in the library. They help students find books. They show students how to search using a computer. They put books away, making sure they're in order. A person who does this job is called a <u>librarian</u>.

Do you know who is in charge of the whole school? That person has a big job. He or she has to make sure that everyone else is doing their jobs. This person has to talk to parents. This person is called the <u>principal</u>.

There are people in the school who keep the school clean. You will see them mopping the floor. You will see them picking up trash. They have to clean the bathrooms. The person who keeps the school clean is called a <u>custodian</u>.

All these people work hard in your school. They work to make the school a safe and clean place for you to learn. The next time you see one of these people, thank them for all the work they do. It will make them happy!

Name_____ **Date** _____

Jobs You See Every Day *(cont.)*

Directions: Read the story on page 83. Then draw a line from the job name to the job picture.

custodian

secretary

principal

bus driver

librarian

crossing guard

Name_____ **Date** _____

When I Grow up, I Want to Be . . .

When you grow up, you will have a job. Have you ever thought about what kind of job you would like to have? In the space below, write about what you would like to be when you grow up. Make sure to begin your sentences with capital letters and end them with periods.

When I grow up, I would like to be _____

_____

_____

_____

_____

_____

_____

_____

_____

Name_____ **Date** _____

Job Interview

In this teacher-directed activity, students interview school staff to find out about the work they do. Consider inviting staff members to class. Allow students to use the questions here or come up with others.

What is your name?

What is your job?

What do you do each day?

What do you like best about your job?

How long have you done this job?

86

Columbus Day
Second Monday in October

Christopher Columbus was an explorer who lived long ago. He was one of the first people to sail from Europe to the "New World." His journey was the first step toward settling our land. On Columbus Day, many people do not have to go to work. There is a big parade in New York City.

Summary of Activities

Reading: Literature
A Mouse's Favorite Day—fictional story with comprehension questions

Reading: Informational Text
Oceans—nonfiction passage with a graphic-organizer activity

Writing
Three Questions for Chris—activity in which students write three questions they have for Christopher Columbus

Bonus
Name Your Fleet—activity in which students color and cut out their own fleet of ships and give them names

Vocabulary: explorer, mammal, nook, parade

Name_____ Date _____

A Mouse's Favorite Day

Directions: Read the story. Then answer the questions on page 89.

Mice love Columbus Day. For them, it is the best day of the year! The first mice that came to the "New World" were brought by Columbus. They snuck onto his ships and sailed across the ocean.

Each year, the mice thank Columbus for what he did, even though he did not mean to do it. First, they have a big parade. They dress up in their best clothes. They make floats out of the bits of trash they find on the ground. They march around and sing songs. Here is one of the songs they sing:

> Oh, CC, thanks from the mice!
>
> We think you are mighty nice.
>
> If you were here, we'd give you a slice
>
> Of our cheesy pie!

After that, the mice have a feast. They bake cheese pie. And they drink cheese tea.

Next, the mice all sit in a circle. This is when they tell mouse tales about how hard it was for those first mice.

"I heard it took eight months to get here!" one mouse squeaks.

"Yes," another says, "and the ship was full of cats!"

All of the mice say, "Yikes!" Mice and cats do not get along.

"Some of us didn't make it," says one mouse sadly.

"True, but most of us did. Hooray!" All of the other mice join in and say, "Hooray!"

At the end of the day, the mice find their nooks and fall to sleep. It has been a fun day. But for mice, Columbus Day always is!

Name_____   Date _____

A Mouse's Favorite Day *(cont.)*

Directions: Read the story on page 88. Then answer the questions.

1. How do you know this story is not true?

    a. Christopher Columbus is not a real person.

    b. Mice do not sing and talk.

    c. Mice have never been on ships.

2. What do the mice do on Columbus Day?

    a. They do tricks.

    b. They sing songs.

    c. They go to school.

3. What is a nook?

    a. a tiny space where mice sleep

    b. something that mice eat

    c. the name of a song that mice sing

Name_____   Date _____

Oceans

Directions: Read the passage. Then complete the activity.

Christopher Columbus sailed across the Atlantic Ocean. Take a look at the map.
Use you finger to trace his route. Read to learn more about the oceans.

Ocean Fact File

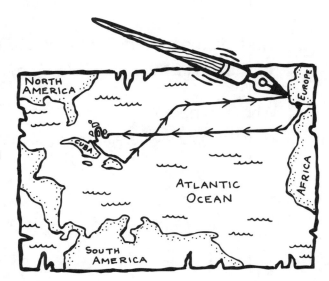

- An ocean is a large body of salty water.
- There are five oceans on Earth.
- The Pacific Ocean is the largest.
- The Arctic Ocean is the smallest.
- Oceans are very deep.
- The sun and the moon cause the ocean to have waves.
- Oceans are full of life.
- Fish live in oceans.
- Mammals, like whales, live in oceans.
- Shellfish, like lobsters, live in oceans.
- The water in the ocean looks bluish-green.
- Most of Earth is covered by oceans.

Activity: Use the Ocean Fact File to help you complete this organizer about oceans.

What Are They?

What Lives in Them?

OCEANS

What Do They Look Like?

Name_____ **Date** _____

Three Questions for Chris

Pretend that you could talk to Christopher Columbus. What would you like to ask him? Write three questions for him in the space below. Make sure to begin your sentences with capital letters and end them with question marks. Remember to use *who, what, when, where, why,* and/or *how.*

Question #1: _____

_____

_____

_____

Question #2: _____

_____

_____

_____

Question #3: _____

_____

_____

_____

Name_____ **Date** _____

Name Your Fleet

Christopher Columbus set sail with a fleet of three ships. They were called the *Niña,* the *Pinta,* and the *Santa María.* Pretend that you are setting sail with a fleet of three ships. Color and cut out your fleet of ships below. Make sure to give each ship a name.

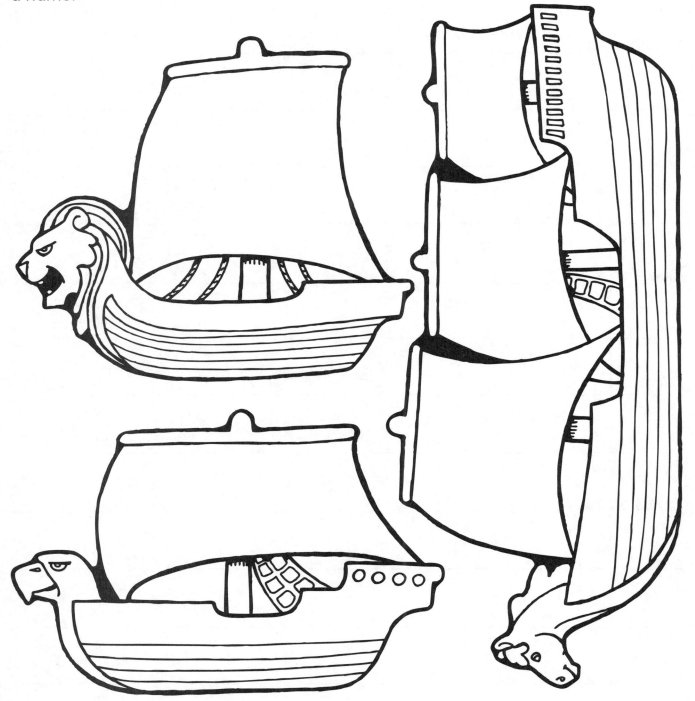

Halloween

October 31

Boo! Did you jump? Are you scared? Halloween is the day of spooky ghosts and mean witches. On Halloween, we dress up in costumes. We go to parties. We march in parades. And we go trick-or-treating for candy! Halloween is a day of make-believe and fun!

Summary of Activities

Reading: Literature
Halloween for Dogs—fictional story with a drawing activity

Reading: Informational Text
How to Roast Pumpkin Seeds—nonfiction passage with comprehension questions

Writing
Dressing Up—activity in which students write about what they want to be for Halloween

Bonus
Pumpkin-Seed Name—activity in which students color and cut out pumpkin seeds and use them to write their names

Vocabulary: costume, parade, pumpkin, silly, spooky, trick-or-treating

Name_____ Date _____

Halloween for Dogs

Directions: Read the story. Then complete the activity.

I have a dog. His name is Bud. Bud is a pit bull. He is light brown. He has really short fur. Some people are afraid of pit bulls. But Bud is not scary at all. He is a very silly dog.

Bud can do tricks. If I throw a stick, he will run to get it and bring it back to me. If I sing a song, he will howl with me. I guess he thinks that he is singing, too! Bud makes my whole family laugh.

Each Halloween, I take Bud with me when I go out trick-or-treating. He loves it! He likes to go from house to house. He gets lots of dog treats. He gets to see some of his dog friends.

The thing Bud likes best about Halloween is that he gets to dress up. Each year, my mom takes us to the pet store. They have lots of costumes for dogs.

Last year, Bud wore a lion costume. He looked great. Another time, he dressed like a bumblebee. He looked silly. This year, Bud will dress like Superman.

I love Bud. Halloween is so much fun with him. Everyone likes to see what Bud will wear. I can't wait for October 31!

Activity: What would you like to see Bud dress up as? Draw a picture of Bud in his costume.

94   ©Teacher Created Resources

Name_____ Date _____

How to Roast Pumpkin Seeds

Directions: Read the passage. Then answer the questions.

In the fall, you will see lots of pumpkins. Pumpkins are a fruit. They are big and round. They are orange. They have brown stems that stick out of the tops. They are heavy.

Inside of each pumpkin, there are seeds. They are good to eat. They make a great snack. But you can't eat them right out of the pumpkin. You have to roast them first. Here's how:

① Scoop the seeds out of the pumpkin.

② Put the seeds in a strainer and rinse.

③ Pat the seeds with a paper towel to dry them off.

④ Put the seeds on a large baking sheet.

⑤ Drizzle olive oil onto the seeds and stir.

⑥ Sprinkle the seeds with salt.

⑦ With adult help, put the seeds in a 350°F oven.

⑧ Roast the seeds for 15 minutes.

⑨ Let the seeds cool off for 5 minutes.

⑩ Eat!

---

1. How long do you roast the seeds?

    a. 5 minutes   **b.** 350 minutes   **c.** 15 minutes

2. What is the sixth thing you do?

    a. Scoop the seeds out of the pumpkin.   **b.** Sprinkle the seeds with salt.   **c.** Eat the seeds.

3. What color is the stem of the pumpkin?

    a. brown   **b.** black   **c.** white

Name_____ **Date** _____

Dressing Up

Think about what you would like to be for Halloween this year. Will it be something scary? Will it be something silly? Will it be something fun? Write about it here. Make sure to begin your sentences with capital letters and end them with periods.

This Halloween, I would like to be _____

_____

_____

_____

_____

_____

_____

_____

_____

_____

Name_____ **Date** _____

Pumpkin-Seed Name

Count how many letters are in your first name. Color that many pumpkin seeds light brown. Write each letter of your name on a seed. Cut out each seed that you colored. Place the seeds on a piece of orange construction paper. Arrange them to spell your name. Paste the seeds to the paper.

Veterans Day
November 11

On Veterans Day, we honor all of the people who have served in the armed forces of our country. Some people have been soldiers in the Army. Others have been sailors in the Navy. People in the military help to keep us safe. They protect our freedom. They serve so that others don't have to. You do not go to school on Veterans Day. Many people do not go to work on this day. It is a day to remember and to say thank you.

Summary of Activities

Reading: Literature
Sue's Big Surprise!—fictional story with a sequencing activity

Reading: Informational Text
Uniforms of the Armed Forces—nonfiction passage with comprehension questions

Writing
Thank You, Veterans—activity in which students write thank-you notes to veterans

Bonus
Branches of the Armed Forces—activity in which students color and cut out the five insignias of the United States Armed Forces

Vocabulary: Air Force, armed forces, Army, Coast Guard, military, Navy, soldiers, uniform, U.S. Marine Corps, veteran, war

Name_____ Date _____

Sue's Big Surprise!

Directions: Read the story. Then complete the activity on page 100.

My mom used to be in the Army. She was a soldier. She is also a nurse. She was in a war. The war was in a place I had never heard of. It was far away. My mom was gone for almost one year. I missed her very much.

Sometimes, I worried about my mom. My dad told me that she was safe. He said that she had a big job to do. She had to take care of people who got hurt. My mom is a great nurse.

One day, my mom gave me the biggest surprise I ever had. It happened at school. I had a part in the school play. The play was about the four seasons. I had the part of the sun. I was dressed all in yellow.

Lots of people came on the day of the play. The room was full of moms and dads. I was sad because I knew my mom was far away. I walked out onto the stage. I started to say my lines.

"I am the sun. I am strong in the summer."

I looked out at all of the people who were watching the play. All of a sudden, I saw my mom! She was sitting right in the middle of the front row! She was smiling. Instead of saying my next line, I said, "Mom! Mom!"

Everyone laughed. My mom ran up onto the stage. She was wearing her uniform. She picked me up. She gave me a big hug. We both cried. People started to clap and take pictures.

My mom walked off of the stage. I said the rest of my lines. The play went well. People clapped for us when it was over. We all took a bow.

I ran off of the stage and into my mom's arms. She would have to leave again. But, for now, we were together.

THANK YOU FOR OUR FREEDOM!

Name_____ Date _____

Sue's Big Surprise! *(cont.)*

Directions: Read the story on page 99. Each of the sentence strips below has part of the story. Cut out each strip. Put the story in order. Paste the strips in the correct order onto a piece of construction paper. Retell the story for classmates.

Sue ran off of the stage into her mom's arms.

Sue's Big Surprise!

Sue walked out onto the stage to say her lines.

Sue was in the school play.

Sue saw her mom sitting in the front row.

Name_____ Date _____

Uniforms of the Armed Forces

Directions: Read the passage. Then answer the questions.

A uniform is a set of clothes that a group of people has to wear. They all look the same. Some students have to wear one at school. Maybe you do, too!

On Veterans Day, you may see people wearing uniforms. They are the special clothes that you wear if you are in the armed forces.

There are five branches, or parts, to the United States Armed Forces. They are:

- Army

- Navy

- Air Force

- U.S. Marine Corps

- Coast Guard

Each branch has its own uniform.

When you join the armed forces, you get two uniforms. One is the kind you wear every day. The other one is called a dress uniform. You wear that one on special days.

On Veterans Day, you may see some veterans that have medals on their uniforms. They earn medals by being brave and helping others.

---

1. The armed forces has _____ branches.
   a. 5   **b.** 3   **c.** 10

2. When does a soldier wear a dress uniform?
   a. every day   **b.** on Sundays   **c.** on special days

3. You can earn a medal if you are
   a. funny.   **b.** brave.   **c.** tall.

Name_____ **Date** _____

Thank You, Veterans

Veterans Day is a time to thank the people in the armed forces who serve our country and help to keep us safe. In the space below, write a thank-you note to all of the veterans. Make sure to begin your sentences with capital letters and end them with periods.

Dear Veterans,

_____

_____

_____

_____

_____

_____

_____

Sincerely,

_____

Name_____ Date _____

Branches of the Armed Forces

There are five branches of the United States Armed Forces. They are the Army, the Navy, the Air Force, the U.S. Marine Corps, and the Coast Guard. Each part has its own special picture that stands for who they are. Look at the pictures below. Color each picture. Then cut them out and mount them onto a piece of construction paper. Make sure to label each one.

Thanksgiving

Fourth Thursday in November

It's turkey time! On Thanksgiving Day, we join with our family and friends to give thanks for the harvest. That's another way of saying that it is a time to be grateful for all of the good food that we have to eat. Most people are off from school and work on Thanksgiving Day. Thanksgiving Day also marks the start of the holiday season.

Summary of Activities

Reading: Literature
Nana's Pumpkin Pie—fictional story with comprehension questions

Reading: Informational Text
One Wild Turkey!—nonfiction passage with a drawing activity

Writing
Thanksgiving-Day Feast—activity in which students write about their favorite holiday dishes

Bonus
Thanksgiving-Day Parade Float—activity in which students make floats for a classroom Thanksgiving-Day parade

Vocabulary: float, grateful, harvest, parade

Name_____   Date _____

Nana's Pumpkin Pie

Directions: Read the story. Then answer the questions.

My nana makes the best pumpkin pies! She makes the pies all by herself. But this year, she hurt her foot, so she asked me to help. My nana sat in the kitchen chair and told me what to do.

"First," she said, "you will need a big mixing bowl." So I got the bowl from the shelf and brought it to where my nana sat.

"OK, now it's time to crack the eggs." I cracked one, two, three eggs into the bowl. "Give them a good mix," Nana said. I mixed the eggs until I saw tiny bubbles on the top.

"Good mixing," she said. "Now, it's time for the sugar." I poured one-half cup of white sugar into the bowl. Then I did the same thing with the brown sugar.

My mom popped her head into the kitchen. "You ladies O.K.?" My nana gave her the thumbs-up.

The last things that I added to the bowl were the pumpkin and cream. The mixture was an orange-brown color. It smelled so good.

"Now it's time to pour," Nana said. I brought the pie shells over to my nana. She poured all of the batter into them one at a time. My mom put the pies into the oven. After a few minutes, the whole room smelled like pumpkin pie!

"I hope they are as good as when you make them," I said.

After the pies came out of the oven, we set them on a shelf and let them cool off. Then my nana cut a small piece of pie. She gave us each a fork.

"Ready?" she asked. "On the count of three. One, two, three!"

We both stuck our forks into the pie at the same time and then put a taste of the pie into our mouths.

"Yum!" we both said. Then we dove in for a second bite!

---

1. Why does Nana need help?
   a. She hurt her foot.   **b.** She hurt her hand.   **c.** She didn't like to make the pies by herself.

2. How many eggs are in the pie?
   a. 4   **b.** 1   **c.** 3

3. Who put the pies into the oven?
   a. Nana   **b.** Mom   **c.** the person telling the story

Name_____   Date _____

One Wild Turkey!

Directions: Read the passage. Then complete the activity.

There are two kinds of turkeys. There is the kind that we eat on Thanksgiving Day. Then there are wild turkeys. We don't eat this kind.

Wild turkeys live in the woods. They walk along the ground to find food. They like to eat seeds and nuts. They eat grass. They also eat some insects. Wild turkeys can also fly but not too far.

A male turkey is called a tom. He is covered in feathers. They are brown and black. A tom has tail fathers that spread out like a big fan. Look at the tom below. Do you see his tail feathers?

A tom's head and beak are red. A tom has a piece of skin that hangs down from his throat. This is called a wattle. It is red. These parts of the tom don't have any feathers.

A wild turkey makes a funny sound. It is called a gobble. Turkeys can also cluck.

Activity: Follow the instructions to draw a picture.

1. Draw a picture around the tom to show where he lives.
2. Draw some of the food that the tom eats.
3. Color the tom's head, beak, and wattle red.
4. Color the tom's feathers brown and black.

Name_____ **Date** _____

Thanksgiving-Day Feast

On Thanksgiving, most people eat turkey with dressing, pumpkin pie, and lots of other tasty things. In the space below, write about your favorite Thanksgiving dishes. Make sure to begin your sentences with capital letters and end them with periods.

_____

_____

_____

_____

_____

_____

_____

_____

_____

_____

Name_____ **Date** _____

Thanksgiving-Day Parade Float

Each year on Thanksgiving Day, there are parades. In the parades, there are giant floats. Floats are big balloons that are shaped like story or cartoon characters.

Pretend you can make a float of your favorite character for a big Thanksgiving-Day Parade. Who would it be? Draw a picture of it here and color it. Next, cut it out. Attach your float to a craft stick. Set up a mini Thanksgiving-Day parade in your classroom.

Note to Teachers: Use this opportunity to explain the multiple meanings of the word *float*.

Hanukkah

Sometime Between Late November and December

Happy Hanukkah! This day is celebrated by Jews all over the world. Hanukkah is also called the Festival of Lights. Jewish people believe that, a long time ago, an oil lamp was kept lit in a temple for eight nights with only very little oil. They think of this as a miracle. During Hanukkah, Jews light the menorah, spin the dreidel, and eat fried food.

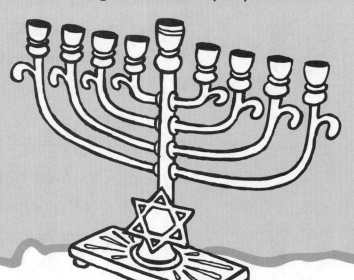

Summary of Activities

Reading: Literature
How Do You Spell . . . ?—a poem with a phonological-awareness activity

Reading: Informational Text
The Dreidel—nonfiction passage with comprehension questions

Writing
Giving to Others—activity in which students write about how they might help others

Bonus
Making a Menorah—activity in which students make menorahs out of their handprints

Vocabulary: culture, dreidel, Hebrew, Jewish, Judaism, miracle

Name_____   Date _____

How Do You Spell . . . ?

Directions: Read the poem. Then complete the activity.

Some people start off with an H

And others with a C.

It can end with H or A.

It's as muddled as can be!

H, A, two Ns, and then a U

A K another A,

It's easy to remember,

If you practice every day.

Or C H A N U K A H

It starts with another letter,

Begin with H or with a C,

Who's to say which one is better?

And don't forget the one

That has the double Ks,

When you're playing with your dreidel,

On these very special days.

There are many different ways to spell

This Festival of Lights.

Just stick with one of these,

And you'll always know you're right!

Activity:

1. Look at the last word or letter in each line. Draw a circle around the ones that rhyme. Draw a box around the ones that don't.

2. Use the clues in the poem to write on the back of the page the three ways to spell the Festival of Lights.

Name_____   Date _____

The Dreidel

Directions: Read the passage. Then answer the questions.

On Hanukkah, you can play a game with a dreidel. A dreidel is a toy. It is traditionally made of wood. A dreidel is a top that spins. Look at the dreidel in the picture. Can you see the little stem on the top? You use that to spin the dreidel.

The dreidel has four sides. Each side has a letter on it. The letters are from the Hebrew alphabet.

- The letter נ says *Nun*.
- The letter ג says *Gimel*.
- The letter ה says *Hei*.
- The letter ש says *Shin*.

Here's how to play:

- Each player puts 10 pieces in the pot. A piece can be one raisin or one jellybean.
- Each player takes a turn to spin the dreidel.
- If נ is facing up, the player does nothing.
- If ג is facing up, the player gets everything in the pot.
- If ה is facing up, the player gets half of the pieces.
- If ש is facing up, the player adds three pieces to the pot.
- If you run out of pieces, you are out of the game.
- The person with the most pieces wins!

---

1. What letter is showing in the picture above?
    a. Gimel   b. Shin   c. Nun

2. How do you win a game of dreidel?
    a. run out of pieces   b. have the most pieces   c. get ה five times

3. How many sides does a dreidel have?
    a. 3   b. 2   c. 4

Name_____ **Date** _____

Giving to Others

On Hanukkah, many children are encouraged to give to others who need help. Think about how you might be able to help someone else. Write down three ways below. Make sure to end your sentences with periods.

1. **I could help others by** _____

_____

_____

_____

2. **I could help others by** _____

_____

_____

_____

3. **I could help others by** _____

_____

_____

_____

Name_____ **Date** _____

Making a Menorah

The menorah is a big part of Hanukkah. A menorah is a candleholder. It has a place for nine candles. One candle is lit each evening for eight nights. Here is a fun way to make a menorah of your own.

You will need these items:

- large piece of white construction paper
- pencil
- crayons
- scissors

Here are the steps to making a menorah:

1. Place your left pointer finger down in the middle of the white paper.

2. Trace your pointer finger with a pencil.

3. Place your left hand down on the paper next to the pointer finger that you just traced.

4. Trace your left hand with a pencil. Do not include your thumb.

5. Place your right hand down on the paper next to the pointer finger you traced earlier.

6. Trace your right hand with a pencil. Do not include your thumb.

7. Color the fingertips of your traced hands yellow for the candle flame.

8. Color the rest of your menorah.

9. Cut out your menorah.

Christmas

December 25

Merry Christmas! This day is celebrated by Christians all over the world. Christians believe that this is the day that Jesus Christ was born. On this day, Christians go to church and spend time with family and friends. Christmas is also a time to give gifts, decorate houses with lights, and visit with Santa Claus.

Summary of Activities

Reading: Literature
One Last Thing—fictional story with comprehension questions

Reading: Informational Text
Reindeer—nonfiction passage with a drawing activity

Writing
My Favorite Toy—activity in which students write about their favorite toys

Bonus
Making a Tree Ornament—activity in which students make ornaments

Vocabulary: Christian, Christianity, decorate, garland, ornament, reindeer, Santa Claus, sleigh, stockings

Name_____ Date _____

One Last Thing

Directions: Read the story below and on page 116. Then answer the questions on page 116.

It was 8 o'clock on Christmas Eve. Pete and his dad hung the last ball on the tree.

"It looks great, Dad," Pete said.

"It sure does. I think it's the best tree ever."

Pete and his dad stood there for a minute and watched the lights on the tree twinkle. Then, Pete picked up two red Christmas stockings. He handed one to his dad.

"Time to hang the stockings, Dad."

Pete's dad took both stockings over to the Christmas tree. He laid them down around the bottom of the tree.

"We don't really have anywhere to hang them," he said.

"Do you think Santa Claus will find them down here?" Pete asked.

"Sure he will. He's Santa!"

Pete looked around. He looked at the Christmas tree. He looked at the stockings.

"I think we are ready for Santa," he said to his dad.

"Mostly," Pete's dad said. "But there's one last thing we have to do."

"Really?" Pete said. "What's that?"

"Do you remember how Santa gets around?"

"He rides a sleigh, right?" Pete asked.

"Yes, but what pulls Santa's sleigh?"

"Oh, right!" Pete remembered. "Flying reindeer!"

Pete went to the kitchen to get a big bowl. He put carrots and lettuce into the bowl. He also put in some celery and green bell peppers.

"Where should we put it?" Pete asked.

"How about out on the front lawn?"

"O.K. But just in case, I'm going to write a letter to Santa."

Name_____ **Date** _____

One Last Thing *(cont.)*

Directions: Read the story beginning on page 115. Then answer the questions.

Pete went and got a marker and a piece of paper. This is what he wrote:

Dear Santa,
Here is some food for your reindeer. We hope they like it! Merry Christmas!
Pete and Jim

Pete took the reindeer food outside. He put the letter to Santa right next to it. He put a small rock on top, so the note would not blow away.

"Are we ready for Santa now?" Pete asked his dad.

"Mostly," he said. "There's just one last thing."

Pete smiled. "I know, Dad. I know."

Pete kissed his dad. Then he walked up the stairs and went to bed.

---

1. Why does Pete feed the reindeer carrots and lettuce?
   a. It was the only food they had in the house.
   b. It is what reindeers like to eat.
   c. The reindeer were on a diet.

2. What is the name of Pete's dad?
   a. Tom
   b. Sam
   c. Jim

3. What does Pete put on top of his note to Santa?
   a. a rock
   b. his stocking
   c. the reindeer food

Name_____   Date _____

Reindeer

Directions: Read the passage. Then complete the activity on page 118.

Reindeer live in cold places. They have lots of special things about them that help them live where it is cold.

The Fur of the Reindeer

Reindeer have two coats of fur. One is called the undercoat. This is the coat of fur that is close to the skin. It is very thick. On top of that, there is another coat of fur. The fur that is on the outside of the reindeer is longer. Two coats of fur keep the reindeer very warm.

The fur of a reindeer can be white. It can also be light brown or even very dark brown.

The Nose of the Reindeer

Reindeer have big noses. They can breathe in lots of air in a single breath. The air is warmed inside of their noses. By the time the air gets to the lungs, it is nice and toasty. This helps the reindeer live in cold places.

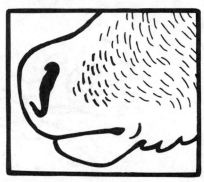

The Feet of the Reindeer

Reindeer have hooves. Hooves are part of the feet. Hooves are the toes of the reindeer. They have very hard, big nails. These hooves help the reindeer to walk on hard, icy ground.

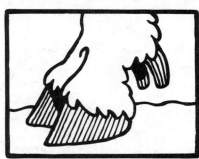

The Antlers of the Reindeer

Antlers are on the top of a reindeer's head. They are made of bone. They always grow in pairs. The bigger the antlers are, the older the reindeer is. Sometimes, reindeer use their antlers when they fight.

Name_____ **Date** _____

Reindeer *(cont.)*

Directions: Read the passage on page 117. Use what you learned about reindeer to complete this drawing. Follow these instructions:

1. Color the antlers brown.

2. Color the hooves black.

3. Draw the reindeer nose and color it red.

4. Color the fur white and brown.

When you are finished, make sure to label each part of the reindeer.